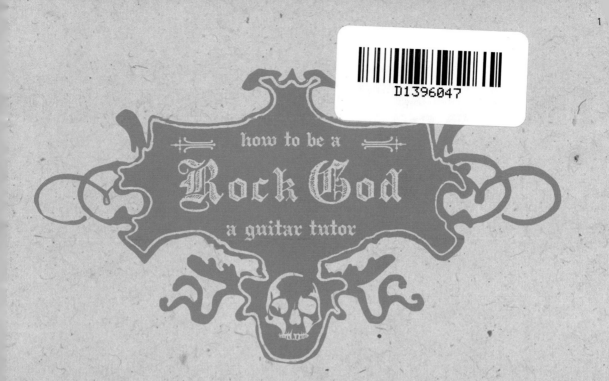

how to be a

Rock God

a guitar tutor

© 2007 by Faber Music Ltd
First published by Faber Music Ltd in 2007
3 Queen Square, London WC1N 3AU

Written by Dr Rock
Riffs by Dr Rock & Olly Weeks
Edited by Lucy Holliday & Kathryn Knight

Designed by Lydia Merrills-Ashcroft
Illustrated by LAMB

Thanks to Wyvern Bindery
Special thanks to Pate, Edd & Jake

Printed in England by Caligraving Ltd
All rights reserved

ISBN10: 0-571-52910-0
EAN13: 978-0-571-52910-0

To buy Faber Music publications or to find out about the full range of titles available,
please contact your local music retailer or Faber Music sales enquiries:

Faber Music Ltd, Burnt Mill, Elizabeth Way, Harlow, CM20 2HX England
Tel: +44(0)1279 82 89 82 Fax: +44(0)1279 82 89 83
sales@fabermusic.com fabermusic.com

AT THE GIG...

MO'S FAVOURITE ROCK BAND WERE AMAZING!

MO WAS DETERMINED TO BE ROCK'S FUTURE GUITAR HERO

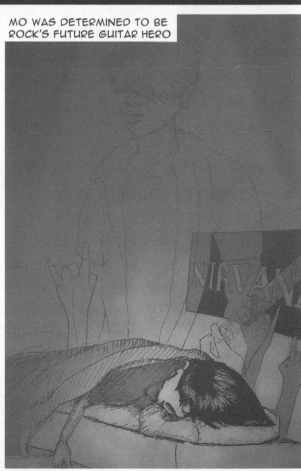

NEXT MORNING HE SPED DOWN
TO HIS LOCAL MUSIC SHOP

...ALONG WITH A TUNER

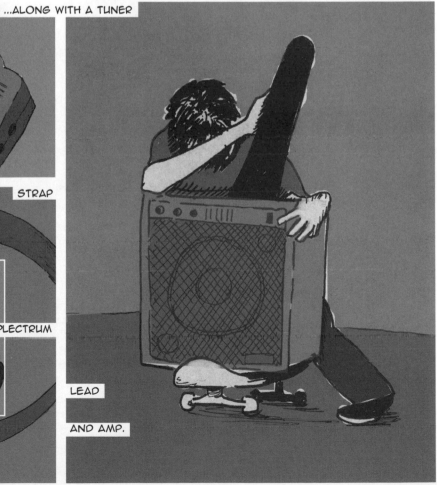

STRAP

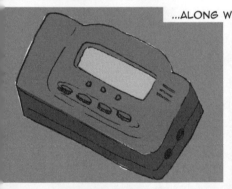

PLECTRUM

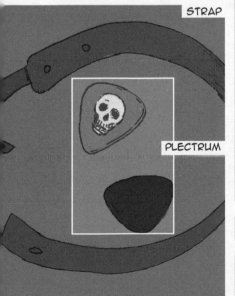

LEAD

AND AMP.

NOW READY TO ROCK, MO PLAYED HIS GUITAR FOR THE FIRST TIME...

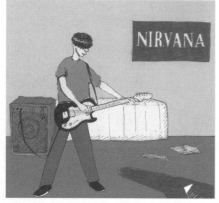

MO WAS DISAPPOINTED, BUT...

...THE SOUND WAS TERRIBL

HE KNEW THERE WA MORE TO KNOW

...BUT WHERE TO START?

...WHAT'S THIS?

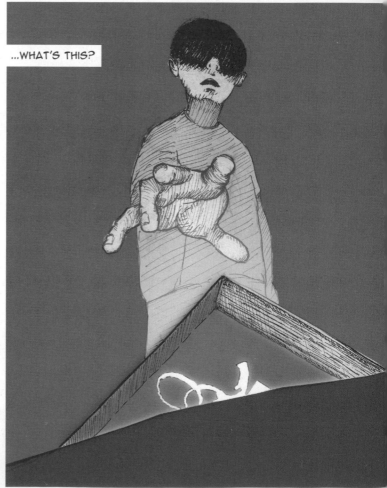

Dear Rock Novice

The future of rock music lies in your hands.
It is up to you to take up the challenge
and create the next generation of rocking music
that will astound mankind.

This book won't teach you every detail.
To be a rock god you need to experiment and
try out different sounds and ways of playing
to suit you.

Jimi Hendrix played his guitar restrung and
turned upside down, Eddie Van Halen popularised
the art of 'tapping', Queen's Brian May built his
own guitar from a bicycle saddle bag, knitting
needle, bits of a motorbike and wood from a 19th
century fireplace. What will you do?

You can become guitar's next hero.

Let us begin.

Dr. Rock

Contents:

*"IT'S GONNA TAKE A PERSON, AND I DON'T KNOW WHO THIS IS,
TO COME ALONG AND REINVENT THE GUITAR AS A VIRTUOSIC INSTRUMENT
IN A COMPLETELY DIFFERENT REALM THAN ANY OF US HAVE DONE,
OR ANYBODY ELSE IN THE PAST. THAT'S THE CLINCHER.
MAYBE THAT WILL HAPPEN AND MAYBE IT WON'T..."*

(Steve Vai)

Rock Music

The first lesson of rock is to listen. Listen to as much music as possible: it will all influence you and will help you with every part of your guitar playing, from rhythm and solos to gurning and extraordinary rock moves. This time line shows a good listening guide to rock, although don't forget the other styles of music too: sometimes the best songs are fusions of different styles.

THE BEACH BOYS
THE BEATLES
DAVID BOWIE
ERIC CLAPTON (CREAM)
DEEP PURPLE
JIMI HENDRIX
THE KINKS
LED ZEPPELIN
PINK FLOYD
THE ROLLING STONES
T. REX
THE WHO

BON JOVI
THE CULT
THE CURE
DEF LEPPARD
GUNS N' ROSES
METALLICA
NIRVANA
PRINCE
RED HOT CHILI PEPPERS
R.E.M.
THE SMITHS
SPINAL TAP
THE STONE ROSES

ARCTIC MONKEYS
THE AUTOMATIC
BLOC PARTY
COLDPLAY
KAISER CHIEFS
KASABIAN
THE KILLERS
THE LIBERTINES
MY CHEMICAL ROMANCE
RAZORLIGHT
THE STROKES
THE TWANG
THE VIEW

1950
1960
1970
1980
1990
2000

CHUCK BERRY
BILL HAYLEY & THE COMETS
BUDDY HOLLY
ELVIS PRESLEY
IKE TURNER
HANK WILLIAMS

AC/DC
AEROSMITH
BLACK SABBATH
BLONDIE
KATE BUSH
THE CLASH
DIRE STRAITS
VAN HALEN
IRON MAIDEN
THE JAM
JOY DIVISION
KISS, MOTORHEAD
QUEEN, THE RAMONES
THE SEX PISTOLS
PATTI SMITH
BRUCE SPRINGSTEEN
THIN LIZZY

BLUR
GREEN DAY
LENNY KRAVITZ
MANIC STREET PREACHERS
MUSE
OASIS
PEARL JAM
PULP
RADIOHEAD
SOUNDGARDEN
SUPERGRASS
THE VERVE
THE WHITE STRIPES

...AND FUTURE STAR, 'MO'!

"FOR THOSE ABOUT TO ROCK WE SALUTE YOU"
(AC/DC)

The Electric Guitar

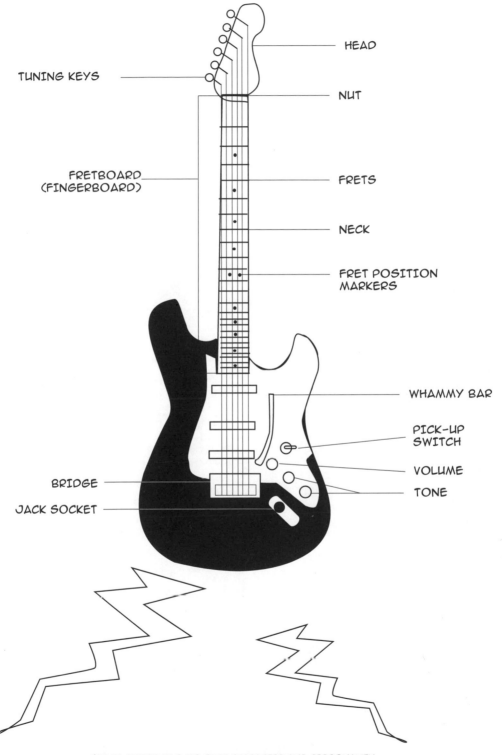

HEAD

TUNING KEYS

NUT

FRETBOARD
(FINGERBOARD)

FRETS

NECK

FRET POSITION
MARKERS

WHAMMY BAR

PICK-UP
SWITCH

VOLUME

TONE

BRIDGE

JACK SOCKET

*"EACH GUITAR HAS ITS OWN CHARACTER AND PERSONALITY,
WHICH CAN BE MAGNIFIED ONCE THE PLAYER ENGAGES IN BEATIN' IT UP!"*
(Billy F. Gibbons - *ZZ Top*)

Tuning Up

Every time you play your guitar, you must make sure it is in tune. Each string has its own pitch.

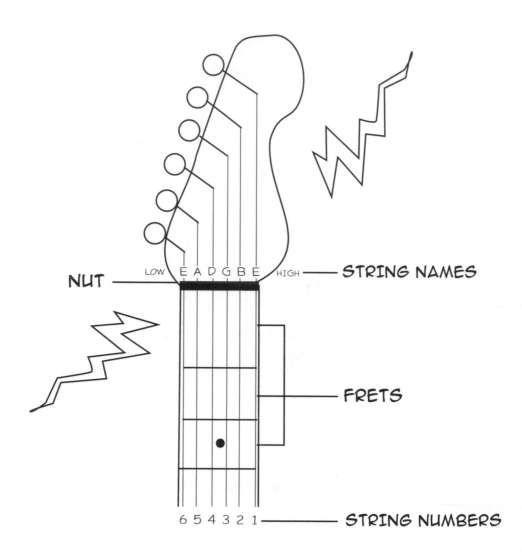

NUT — LOW **E A D G B E** HIGH — **STRING NAMES**

FRETS

6 5 4 3 2 1 — **STRING NUMBERS**

An **electric tuner** (chromatic) is the most reliable way to tune up. Plug your guitar lead straight into the tuner and play a string. The tuner will automatically show you the name of the string you are tuning. Turn your tuning keys up or down until the tuner indicates the correct pitch.

Alternatively, you can tune the guitar into itself by using **relative tuning**. Fret the low 'E' string (string 6) at the 5th fret and pluck. Compare this with the sound of the open 'A' string (5). The two notes should be in tune: if not, adjust the tuning of the 'A' string until the two notes match. Repeat this process for the other strings, apart from the 'G' string, which should be tuned against the 'B' string at fret 4. As a final check, ensure that the bottom and top 'E' strings are in tune with each other. *This diagram shows where to place your fingers.*

E A D G B E

When you play with other people, you must make sure you're in tune with one another.

Reading Chord Boxes

A chord is where you play more than one note at the same time. The chord box is a diagram of the neck and strings of the guitar, showing where you put your fingers and at which fret.

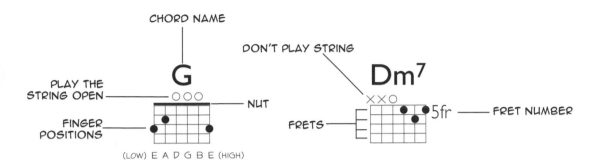

An 'o' means an open string.
The string should be played without your fingers pressing anything on the fretboard.

STRUMMING

You play a chord by strumming the strings. A 'down strum' (↓) means you start at the top (low 'E' (string 6) first), and play downwards. An 'up strum' (↑) means the opposite.

If you are right handed, your right hand should be your 'strumming hand', and your left your 'fretting hand'.

Your fingernails on the fretting hand should be short to make it easier to press the strings down.

THE PLECTRUM (OR PICK)

Use this to play the strings. It gives more power than just your fingertips.
Hold it between your thumb and index finger with the pointed end
striking the strings.

"WHEN YOU STRUM A GUITAR YOU HAVE RHYTHM, BASS, LEAD AND MELODY."
(David Gilmore - *Pink Floyd*)

Reading Tablature 'Tab'

There is no standard music notation in this book. Guitar tab simply shows at which fret your fingers should be, the rhythm and which strings to play.

The numbers indicate the fret, and the 6 lines indicate the strings on the guitar.
The vertical lines represent bar lines.

If there is no marking on one of the strings, this means the string should not be played.
(In a chord box this is indicated by an 'x'.)

An average electric guitar has 22 frets, so the tab number will tell you where to play on the guitar anywhere between 1—22. Here are some examples written in tab and shown as chord boxes:

There are no tempo markings in this book. These would indicate at what speed you should play each riff. When you're learning, it's important to take things slowly, then speed up as you get used to the riffs. Play them at a speed that suits you, then decide for yourself if they sound better faster or slower.

THE 'G' CHORD

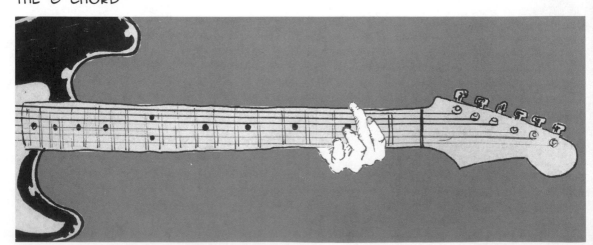

Time Signatures & Rhythm

You've got to have rhythm to rock, and most of the time it will come instinctively, but here are the basics of how to read rhythm in this book.

4/4 :
two beats in each bar,
each beat a 1/2 note

A beat is the natural pulse in a piece of music. Most rock songs are written in 4/4. The top 4 indicates that there are 4 beats in every bar, and the bottom 4 indicates that this beat is a quarter note (crotchet).

OTHER COMMON TIME SIGNATURES

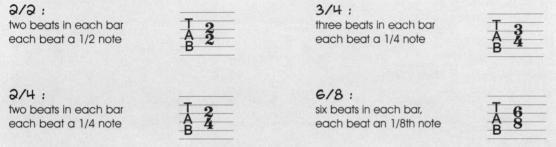

2/2 :
two beats in each bar
each beat a 1/2 note

3/4 :
three beats in each bar
each beat a 1/4 note

2/4 :
two beats in each bar
each beat a 1/4 note

6/8 :
six beats in each bar,
each beat an 1/8th note

NOTES & CORRESPONDING RESTS

Each note duration has a corresponding rest where nothing is played.

Rest

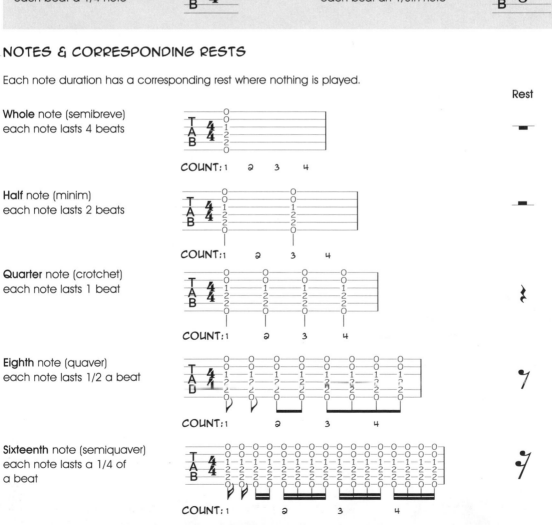

Whole note (semibreve)
each note lasts 4 beats

COUNT: 1   2   3   4

Half note (minim)
each note lasts 2 beats

COUNT: 1   2   3   4

Quarter note (crotchet)
each note lasts 1 beat

COUNT: 1   2   3   4

Eighth note (quaver)
each note lasts 1/2 a beat

COUNT: 1   2   3   4

Sixteenth note (semiquaver)
each note lasts a 1/4 of
a beat

COUNT: 1   2   3   4

Rhythm Exercises

RHYTHM EXERCISE 1

Try playing this rhythm. Count to 4 in your head, maybe in time with the second hand on a watch or clock, then play the chord below using the rhythms as indicated. The notes marked '0' are played open.

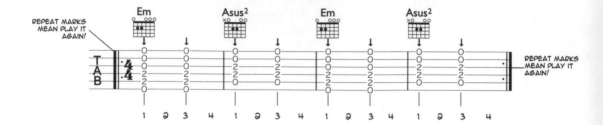

Play each chord with a down strum (↓)

RHYTHM EXERCISE 2

Now try the same chords using different rhythms.

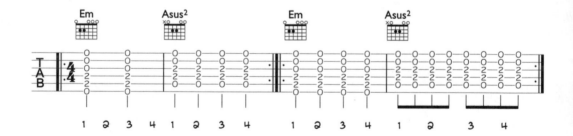

RHYTHM EXERCISE 3

Be careful not to let any other string sound apart from the low 'E' and 'A'.

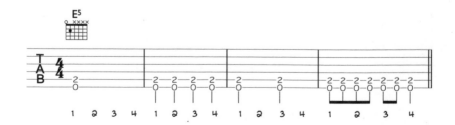

DOTTED RHYTHMS

A dot increases the time value of the note or rest by half. So if a crotchet lasts one beat, adding a dot increases the note length to one and a half beats.

Saying '*and*' between the beat numbers can help to pick out the rhythm of the half beats.

RHYTHM EXERCISE 4

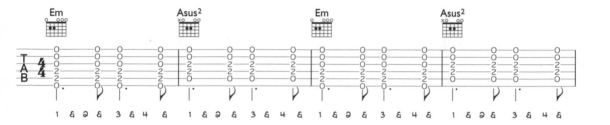

Loads of guitarists keep their rhythm by tapping their foot along with the beat.

The Power Chord

in order to truly rock, you must be a master of the power chord. These are made up of just two notes, and they are indicated with a '5' after the chord name.

After you've mastered the riffs in this section, you'll be well on your way to becoming a rock god...

RIFFS

A riff is a repeated chord progression.

"GIVE ME A RIFF THAT MAKES A KID WANT TO GO OUT AND BUY A GUITAR AND LEARN TO PLAY..."
(Ozzy Osbourne)

PRACTICE POWER RIFF 1

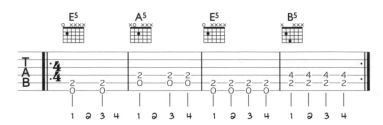

Try playing it again, a little faster.

"I JUST STARTED WRITING SONGS ON MY OWN –
ONCE YOU KNOW THE POWER CHORD YOU DON'T NEED TO KNOW ANYTHING ELSE."
(Kurt Cobain)

PRACTICE POWER RIFF 2

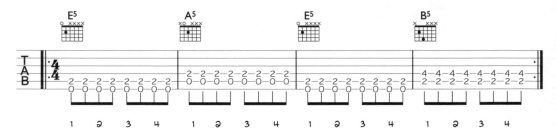

Experiment with the controls and switches on your guitar and amplifier to change the sound, volume and tone.

"NOTHING BEATS A GUITAR THROUGH AN AMP"
(James Hetfield - *Metallica*)

PRACTICE POWER RIFF 3

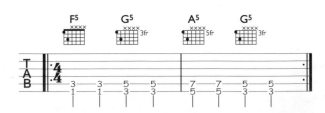

Keep your fingers in the same position and slide up and down the fretboard following the numbers.

Look at the dots on the side of the fretboard, they help you find the right fret:

BOULEVARD OF BROKEN DREAMS
Green Day (from *American Idiot*)

This is the intro to 'Boulevard Of Broken Dreams' from Green Day's massive album, *American Idiot*. Try playing it.

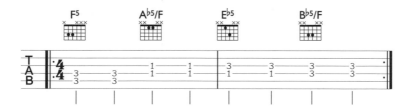

WARNING: to really sound like the record you need a synchronized gate effect, or a note delay effect. If you have neither, just use your rock imagination...

Notice the slash chords here. This is where the lowest note of the chord (bass note) is **not** the 'root' note. The root of a chord is always the name of the chord. So the root of the $A^\flat$ chord would be $A^\flat$, and so on.

PRACTICE POWER RIFF 4

Try not to let your strings ring on in the rest. If you need to mute them, gently rest your strumming hand on the strings to stop them ringing.

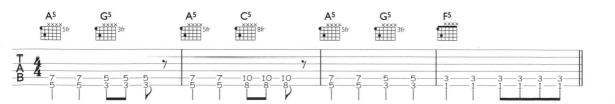

Drop 'D' Tuning

It is common for rock guitarists to tune the low 'E' string (string 6) down to a 'D' as it makes power chords so easy to play. Turn your tuning key for the low 'E' down so that the sound matches the 'D' string (string 4) on the guitar.

This is usually indicated above the tab stave by 6=D.

PRACTICE DROP 'D' RIFF 1

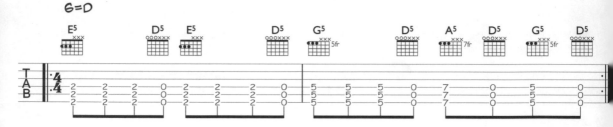

Slide your fingers up and down the fretboard – start slowly then speed up as you get used to the riff.

PRACTICE DROP 'D' RIFF 2

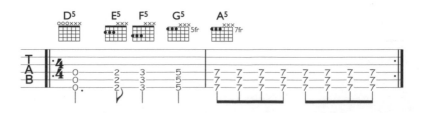

Watch out for the dotted rhythm...

PRACTICE DROP 'D' RIFF 3

Remember to use the dots on the side of the fretboard for this one.

6=D

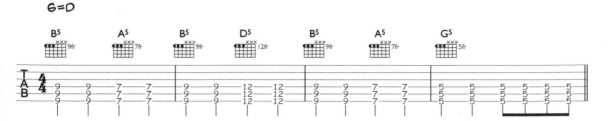

Now re-tune your guitar so the lower string is an 'E' once again.

SMOKE ON THE WATER

Deep Purple (from *Machine Head*)

in 1972, Deep Purple wrote one of the most memorable rock intros of all time using just power chords.

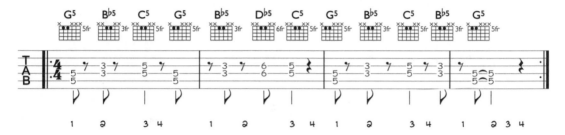

Note the use of a 'tie' in the last bar: its function is to join notes together so they have a longer duration. Often they are used to join notes together across bars.

PRACTICE POWER RIFF 5

This is essentially the same riff as power riff 4, but it has a third string added. The chord is still made up of just two notes, but the root is doubled making the sound all the more powerful.

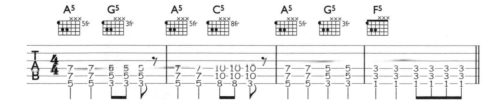

"I TEND TO BE A SUBSCRIBER TO THE IDEA THAT YOU HAVE EVERYTHING YOU NEED BY THE TIME YOU'RE 12 YEARS OLD TO DO INTERESTING WRITING FOR MOST OF THE REST OF YOUR LIFE – CERTAINLY BY THE TIME YOU'RE 18."
(Bruce Springsteen)

RIFF WRITING EXERCISE 1

Try composing your own power chord riff using these chords. Note that apart from the 'E5' chord, all the others use the same shape. Some of the chords won't sound good together in a sequence, but play around, and fit together the ones that sound good to you.

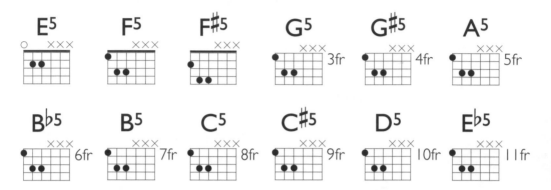

Another common power chord shape uses a different set of 3 strings.
Try chopping and changing between these power chord positions.

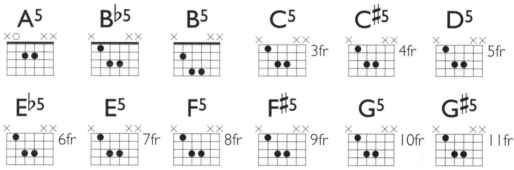

To help get the rhythm tap your foot on the beat.
True rockers would also nod their heads…

Some rockers may 'duck walk' to this riff –
hopping with one leg out in front –
first used by Chuck Berry in the 1950s.

PRACTICE ROCK RIFF 1

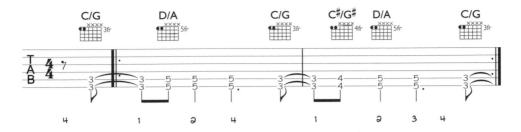

Check out this classic riff written by Yes in 1983:

OWNER OF A LONELY HEART
Yes (from *90125*)

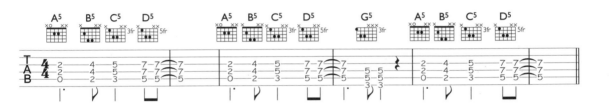

Try and listen to this song before playing the riff. It'll help you pick up the dotted rhythms.

in 2006 Welsh band The Automatic had a big hit with 'Monster'. The chorus is made up of power chords. Try playing it. If you're really confident you could also sing along.

MONSTER
The Automatic (from *Not Accepted Anywhere*)

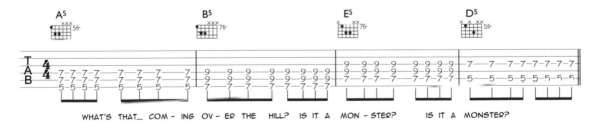

The Top Strings

This time focus on the top three strings. Your fingers should stay in the same position, but move up and down the fretboard following the tab. There are no chord boxes for these riffs in order to help you get used to reading tab.

PRACTICE RIFF 1

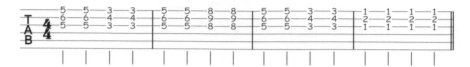

PRACTICE RIFF 2

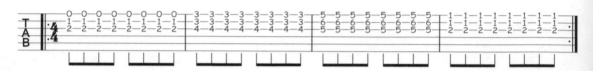

PRACTICE RIFF 3

PRACTICE RIFF 4

PRACTICE RIFF 5

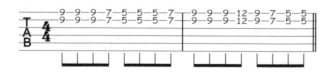

PRACTICE RIFF 6

PRACTICE RIFF 7

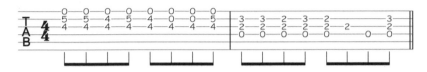

PRACTICE RIFF 8

PRACTICE RIFF 9

PRACTICE RIFF 10

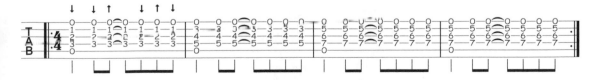

Fret Test

Try out this test to see how well you know your way around the fretboard.
Make sure you play only the top three strings. See how fast you can go!

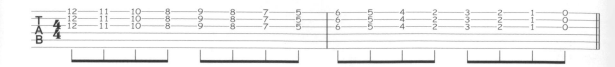

Now try it with strings 3,4 & 5

Rock Licks

A **lick** is a short motif. Licks are great for practising your pick control.

PRACTICE ROCK LICK 1

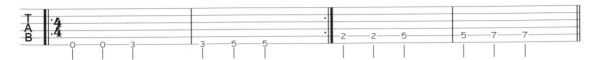

PRACTICE ROCK LICK 2

PRACTICE ROCK LICK 3

PRACTICE ROCK LICK 4

PRACTICE ROCK LICK 5

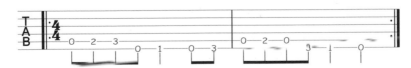

PRACTICE ROCK LICK 6

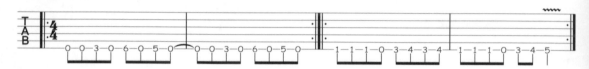

VIBRATO

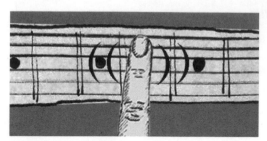

The wavy line in the exercise below indicates **vibrato**. Instrumentalists use vibrato to colour or emphasise a note. To get the effect strike the string and rapidly bend the note with the fretting hand using small up and down movements. Alternatively you can use the **whammy bar** (or tremolo arm), by striking the string then moving the bar up and down quickly. The music will indicate whether to use the bar or not.

PRACTICE ROCK LICK 7

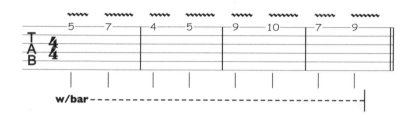

Once you've got how this lick goes, try playing it faster. Note the use of a tie – here, this is held over the bar, so nothing is played on the first beat of bar 2.

PRACTICE ROCK LICK 8

Try this riff using vibrato created by the whammy/tremolo bar. Play the note then wiggle the bar up and down creating the vibrato effect.

COME AS YOU ARE
Nirvana (from *Nevermind*)

Kurt Cobain wrote 'Come As You Are' in 1991, one of the singles from the classic album *Nevermind*.
Here's the intro:

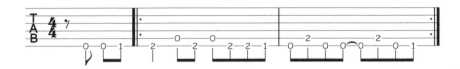

PRACTICE ROCK LICK 9

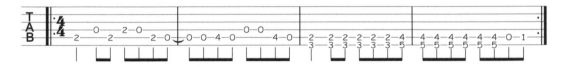

SUNSHINE OF YOUR LOVE
Cream (from *Disraeli Gears*)

The legendary guitarist Eric Clapton often uses **vibrato** in his playing.
Try playing this intro from 1967's 'Sunshine Of Your Love':

The small dots beneath the notes are **staccato** markings.
This means you should make the length of the note as short as possible.

PRACTICE ROCK LICK 10

BREAKING THE LAW

Judas Priest (from *British Steel*)

At the start of the 1980s, Judas Priest released 'Breaking The Law'.
Its intro became one of the most powerful rock licks ever.

FAKE TALES OF SAN FRANCISCO

Arctic Monkeys (from *Whatever People Say I Am, That's What I'm Not*)

In 2006 the Arctic Monkeys became the biggest new guitar band in the UK. The riff from 'Fake Tales Of San Francisco' is great to practise keeping a tight rhythm, and also uses a grace note and slide.

The **Grace Note** is shown as a smaller note, and the **Slide** by a slanted line. A grace note is a quick note that leads up to the note it precedes. It's easy to master. Play the grace note just before the note it is attached to and slide up to that note with your finger without re-striking the string. It is important to keep the rhythm tight, so the grace note is really just an embellishment, or in musical terms an ornament.

Here's the Arctic Monkeys lick:

"ROCK IS SO MUCH FUN.
THAT'S WHAT IT'S ALL ABOUT –
FILLING UP THE CHEST CAVITIES AND EMPTY
KNEECAPS AND ELBOWS."
(Jimi Hendrix)

"gurning"

Slides

SLIDE LICK 1

Slide up or down to the next note without re-striking the string.

SLIDE LICK 2

SLIDE LICK 3

MINI SLIDE PIECE

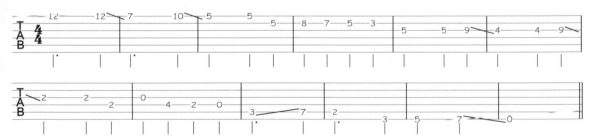

SLIDE RIFF

Keep your fretting hand in the power chord position, and slide up to the next chord without re-striking the strings.

Hammer On

This next lick requires you to use the **hammer on** technique, which is commonly used in rock music. It is always used from a lower note to a higher note. In tab it is indicated by joining the notes together with an arch.

Play the lower note (0), then 'hammer' on to the higher note (2) with another finger, only striking the string once.

• Strike open 'D' string
• Sharply bring index finger down on 'D' string at fret 2
• You should hear a higher note without having to restrike the string

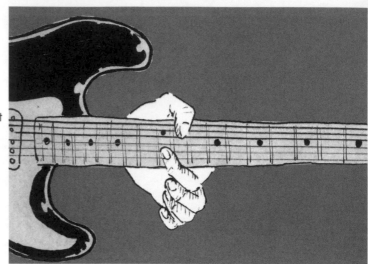

Practise it a couple of times and then try this riff:

HAMMER ON RIFF 1

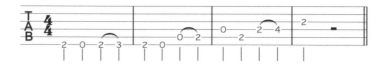

HAMMER ON RIFF 2

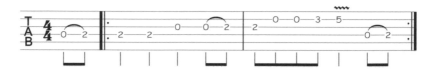

"JIMI HENDRIX CHANGED MY LIFE. EACH GENERATION INFLUENCES THE FOLLOWING ONE, AND AS A CONSEQUENCE BRINGS IT BACK TO THE PAST."
(Robert Smith - *The Cure*)

Pull Off

This is the opposite to a 'hammer on'. This time a higher note is played, and you **pull off** to the lower note with another finger. Again, the string is only struck once.

- Put your middle finger on fret 6
- Put your index finger on fret 5
- Strike the string with the pick
- Remove your middle finger from fret 6 (keeping index finger firmly on fret 5), pulling the string with your middle finger slightly as you remove it.

PULL OFF RIFF 1

PULL OFF RIFF 2

The INXS riff 'Devil Inside' uses a 'pull off'.

DEVIL INSIDE
INXS (from *Kick*)

String Bends

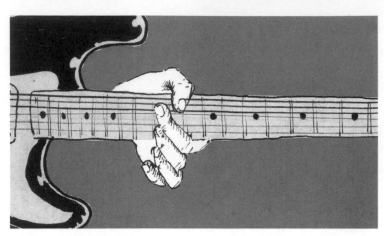

Commonly used in guitar solos and accompanied by a gurn...

Bends are shown by a curved arrow pointing to a tab number.

Fret the first note, and then bend the string up by the amount shown.

A QUARTER-TONE BEND (BLUES CURL)
Bend equivalent to raising the note by roughly half a fret

A HALF STEP BEND
Bend equivalent to raising the note by one fret

A WHOLE STEP BEND
Bend equivalent to raising the note by two frets

BEND AND RELEASE
Bend the string as shown, then release back to the original note.

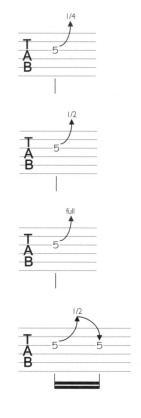

PRACTICE BEND LICK

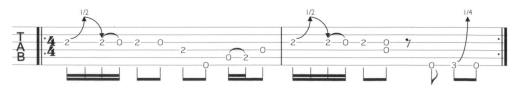

Open Chords

These are full chords in their simplest form on the fretboard. They also use 'open strings'. Using these chord shapes and rhythm slashes try playing these sequences. As you become used to the shapes, start experimenting with your own strumming patterns.

OPEN PATTERN 1

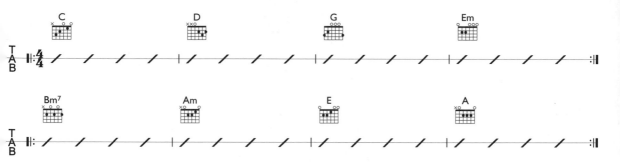

OPEN PATTERN 2

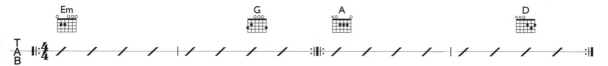

OPEN PATTERN 3

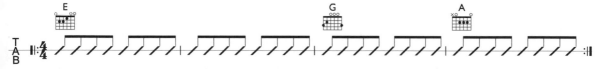

OPEN PATTERN 4

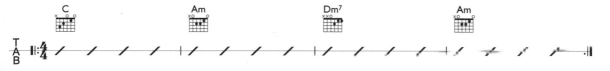

Picking

For these picking patterns, play your guitar with a clean sound (so with no effects or distortion), in order to clearly hear which notes you are playing.

PICKING PATTERN 1

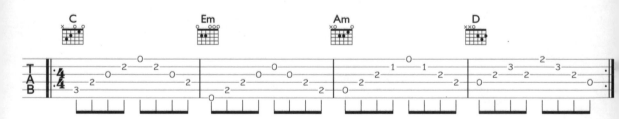

PICKING PATTERN 2

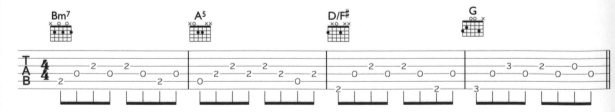

PICKING PATTERN 3

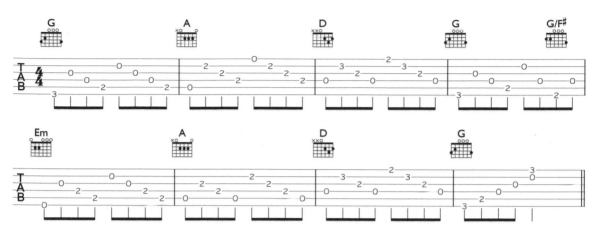

PICKING PATTERN 4

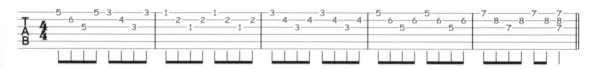

MORE THAN A FEELING
Boston (from *Boston*)

In 1976, the rock group Boston had their biggest hit with 'More Than A Feeling'. Try playing the picked intro. It's helpful to look at the chord shapes first.

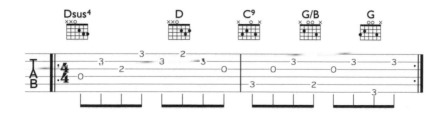

PICKING PATTERN 5

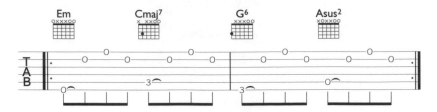

The **Arc** attached to the notes means you should let these notes ring on.

PICKING PATTERN 6

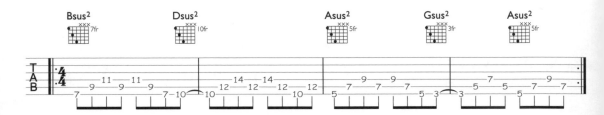

WAKE ME UP WHEN SEPTEMBER ENDS
Green Day (from *American Idiot*)

This rock anthem also has a picked intro:

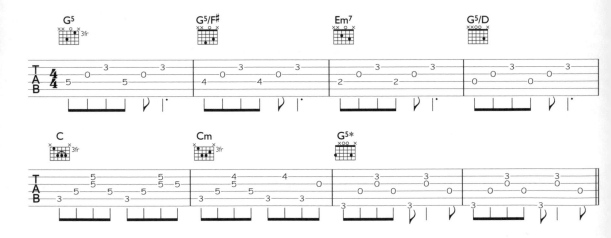

"I LISTENED TO A LOT OF BOB DYLAN'S SONGS, TOM WAITS AND SPRINGSTEEN. I ALWAYS THOUGHT IT WAS IMPORTANT TO BE INTERESTED IN WHAT HAPPENED IN THE PAST."
(Billie Joe Armstrong - Green Day)

Muting

A common way to get a percussive sound out of your guitar is to use a technique called **muting**. Gently lie your fretting finger across all the strings (don't press them down at all) and strike the marked strings. Muted notes are shown as an 'x'. Try this riff:

MUTE PRACTICE RIFF 1

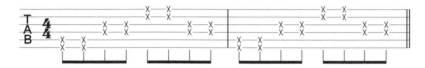

It takes a while to get used to, but keep practising.

MUTE PRACTICE RIFF 2

These riffs use an **accent** (>). This means you should emphasise these chords, by striking them slightly harder than the others so they stand out.

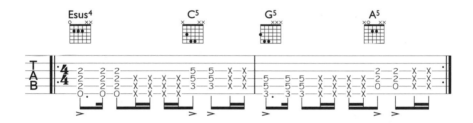

MUTE PRACTICE RIFF 3

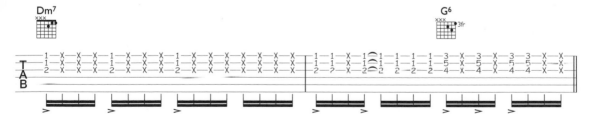

One of the most famous rock songs uses muting as part of the main riff:

SMELLS LIKE TEEN SPIRIT
Nirvana (From *Nevermind*)

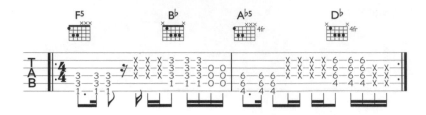

PALM MUTING

This is another way of getting a percussive effect out of your guitar. This time the muting is done with the strumming hand, although it's actually the side of the hand that you use rather than the palm.
Place the side of your hand near the bridge of the guitar and gently touch the strings, just to mute them slightly. You may find it easier than muting with your fretting hand.

The palm muting instruction is indicated with a P.M. beneath the notes.

PALM MUTE RIFF 1

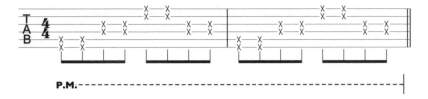

PALM MUTE RIFF 2

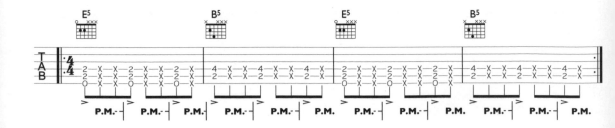

Barre Chords

A **barre chord** is where one finger is used to press down multiple strings across the fretboard. The great thing about these chords is that the same fretting hand positions can be used up and down the fretboard, making fast riffs easier to play.

The index finger 'barres' the strings, effectively becoming the nut.
On a chord box, the barre is represented by a black arc across the strings. e.g:

BARRE CHORD RIFF 1 (SHAPE 1)

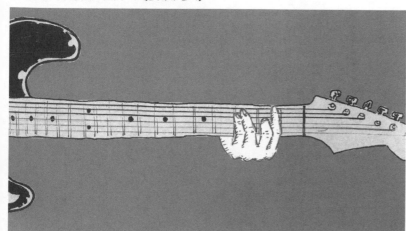

The hardest part of playing these chords is getting your finger to press the strings down hard enough in order to get an even ringing tone when you play the chord. The key is to keep practising…

Make sure your thumb is in line with your barred index finger, and the tips of your other fingers are curled so they fret the strings cleanly.

There are two standard barre shapes for major chords.

BARRE CHORD RIFF 2 (SHAPE 2)

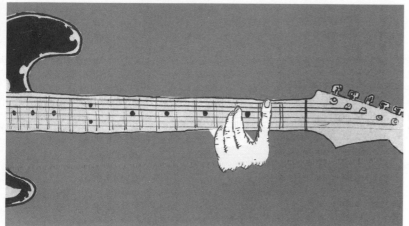

WARNING
Every guitarist finds the 'F' barre chord very difficult to play, so don't worry if it doesn't come easily – it's just one of those things…

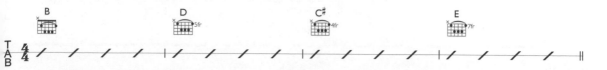

MINOR CHORDS

To play a minor chord shape, you need to change just one finger from the major shape. The minor shape is marked with an 'm' after the chord name.

BARRE SHAPE 1:

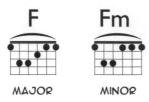

MAJOR   MINOR

BARRE SHAPE 2:

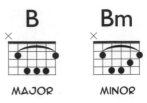

MAJOR   MINOR

BARRE CHORD MINOR RIFF 3 (SHAPE 1)

BARRE CHORD MINOR RIFF 4 (SHAPE 2)

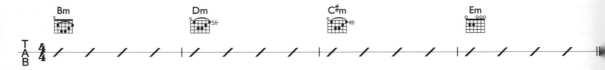

BARRE CHORD RIFF 5

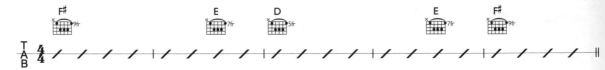

BARRE CHORD RIFF 6

This is how barre chords look in tab:

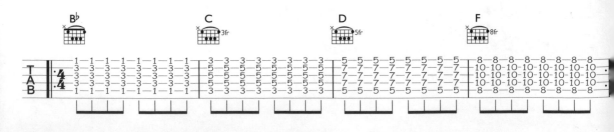

BARRE CHORD RIFF 7

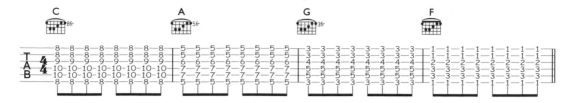

BARRE CHORD RIFF 8

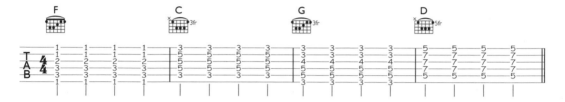

BARRE CHORD RIFF 9

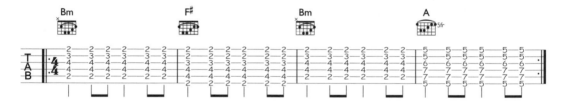

BARRE PICKING RIFF

This exercise is great for checking that you're playing your barre chords cleanly, so each note is heard.

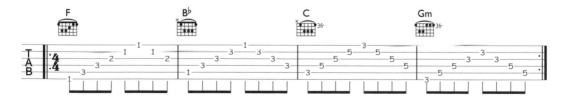

38

Try writing your own chord sequence using these sets of barre chords:

RIFF WRITING EXERCISE 1: BARRE CHORDS (MAJOR KEY) –SHAPE 1

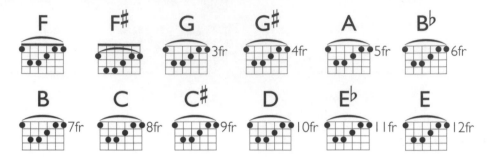

RIFF WRITING EXERCISE 2: BARRE CHORDS (MAJOR KEY) –SHAPE 2

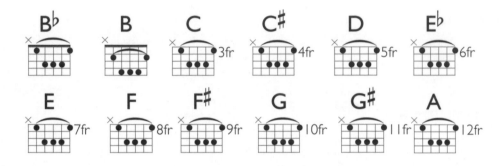

RIFF WRITING EXERCISE 3: BARRE CHORDS (MINOR KEY) –SHAPE 1

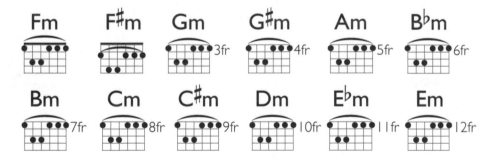

RIFF WRITING EXERCISE 4: BARRE CHORDS (MINOR KEY) –SHAPE 2

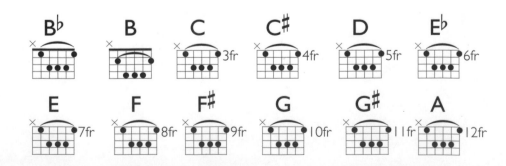

Combining Riffs & Licks

RIFF & LICK 1

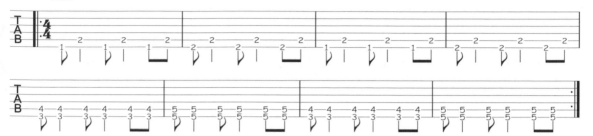

RIFF & LICK 2

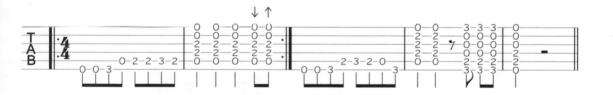

RIFF & LICK 3

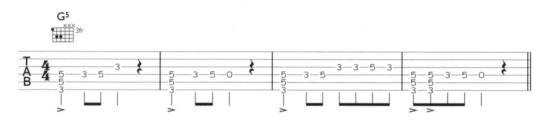

BACK IN BLACK
AC/DC (From Back In Black)

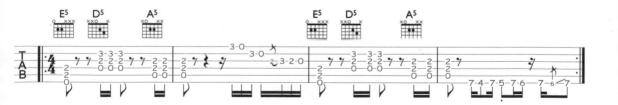

Written in 1980, this is one of the most famous rock riffs ever!
Remember how to play grace notes, slides and staccato.

The Solo

The solo is the part of a song when the lead guitarist reveals his true rock god colours; it provides an excellent opportunity to perform a rock-tastic medley of poses and moves.

Essentially, the solo is a series of licks played over the top of a chord progression in a song. While composing your solo you must make sure that the notes you choose will sound great with the chords underneath. This is a skill that comes with much practice and experimentation but the best way of learning is by listening to some genuine rock legends. Check out the solos in 'Immigrant Song' (Led Zeppelin), 'Paranoid' (Black Sabbath), 'Ace Of Spades' (Motorhead), 'Ain't Talkin' 'Bout Love' (Van Halen), 'Badge' (Cream), 'Sweet Child O' Mine' (Guns n' Roses), 'Exo-politics' (Muse), 'Dancing Shoes' (Arctic Monkeys), 'High And Dry' (Radiohead), 'Back In Black' (AC/DC)… the list is endless!

'LET YOUR FINGERS DO THE ROCKING!'

PRACTICE SOLO

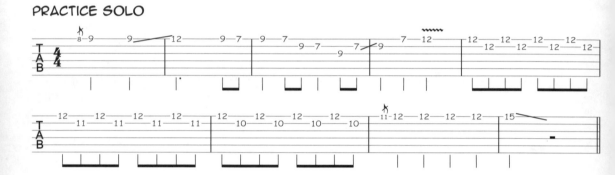

PRACTICE SOLO 2

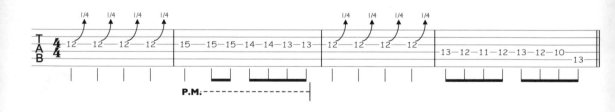

PRACTICE SOLO 3

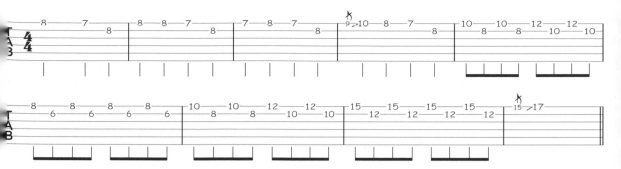

PRACTICE SOLO 4

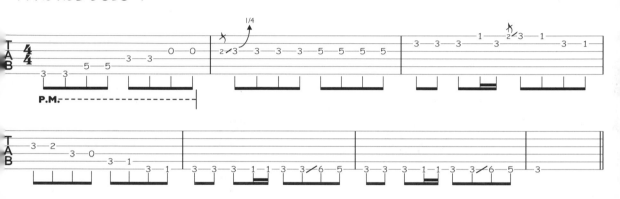

PRACTICE SOLO 5

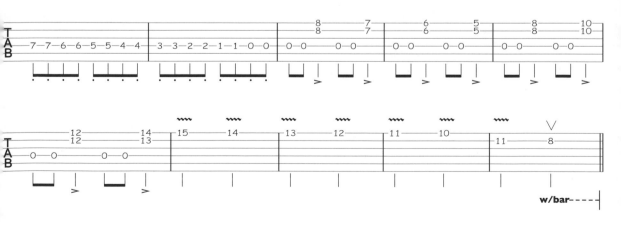

Congratulations. You have just climbed the first rung of the ladder towards Rock Heaven!
If you have any comments on this book, or need any help, email **Dr.Rock@fabermusic.com**

Rock Moves

All rock guitarists develop their own distinctive moves and gurns...
Here are a few of the more famous, if a little silly, rock moves for you to try.

*"I USED TO POSE IN FRONT OF THE MIRROR AT HOME. I WAS HOPEFUL.
THE ONLY THING I WAS LACKING WAS A BIT OF BREAD TO BUY AN INSTRUMENT.
BUT I GOT THE MOVES OFF FIRST, AND I GOT THE GUITAR LATER."*
(Keith Richards - *The Rolling Stones*)

'MACHINE GUN'
see Bruce Springsteen

'POWER STANCE'
HOLD THE 'GOBLET OF ROCK'
see Matt Bellamy
Muse

'WINDMILL'
see Pete Townsend
The Who

"VERTICAL HOLD"
see Jimmy Page
Led Zeppelin

see also:
"DUCK WALK" p24

Chord Dictionary

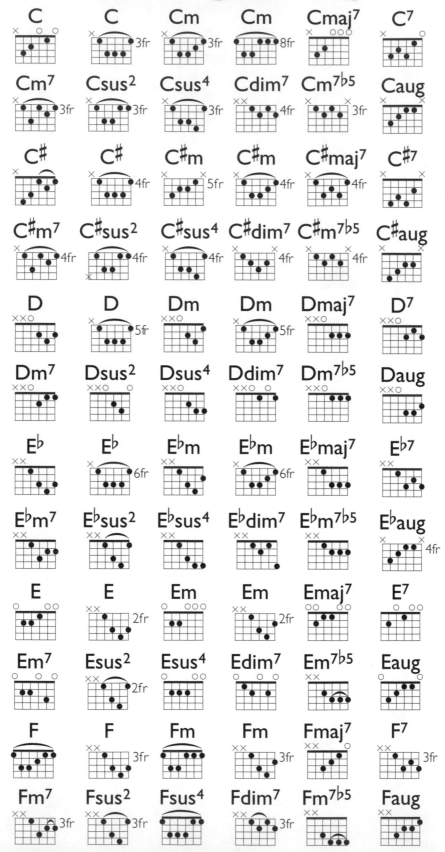

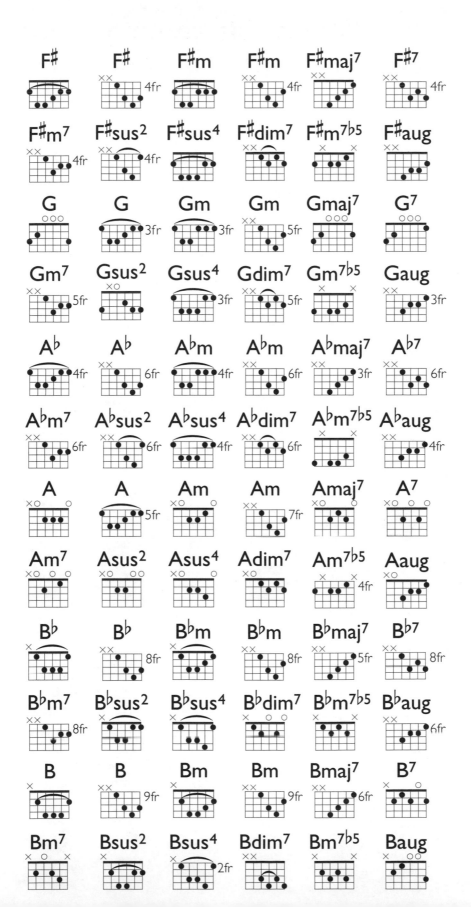

MO WAS EXHAUSTED FROM READING & PRACTISING...

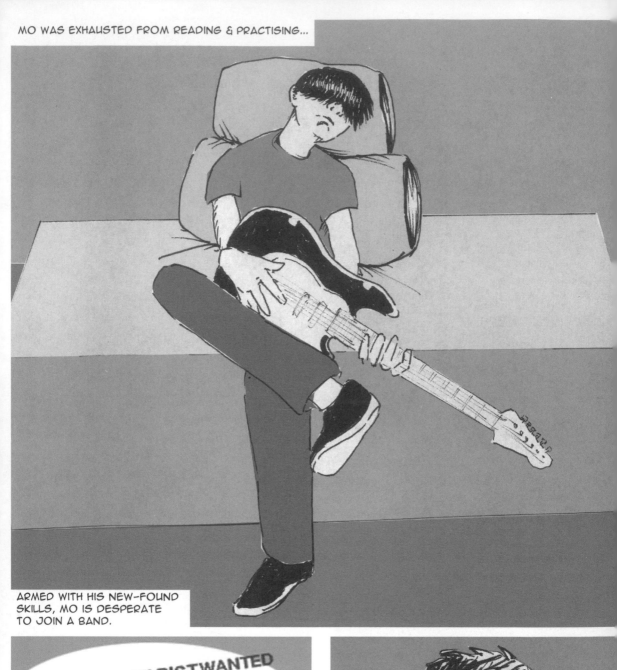

ARMED WITH HIS NEW-FOUND
SKILLS, MO IS DESPERATE
TO JOIN A BAND.

THE END...?